M.O.N.E.Y. MATRIX PRESENTS

PARABLES
FOR
PROFIT
VOL. 1

FACTS TELL—STORIES SELL

WOODY WOODWARD

© 2017 D.U. Publishing All Rights Reserved

Reproduction or translation of any part of this book beyond that permitted by Section 107 or 108 of the 1976 United States Copyright Act without written permission of the copyright owner is unlawful. Criminal copyright infringement is investigated by the FBI and may constitute a felony with a maximum penalty of up to five years in prison and/or a $250,000 fine. Request for permission or further information should be addressed to the Inspirational Product Division, D.U. Publishing.

> D.U. Publishing
> www.dupublishing.com

Warning—Disclaimer

The purpose of this book is to educate and inspire. This book is not intended to give advice or make promises or guarantees that anyone following the ideas, tips, suggestions, techniques or strategies will have the same results as the people listed throughout the stories contained herein. The author, publisher and distributor(s) shall have neither liability nor responsibility to anyone with respect to any loss or damage caused, or alleged to be caused, directly or indirectly by the information contained in this book.

ISBN: 978-0-9982340-3-8

M.O.N.E.Y. Matrix™ is registered trademark of Woody Woodward.

Contents

Introduction iii

If You Do This One Thing Each Day,
You Will Reach Your Goal 3

This Lady Did One Crazy Thing And It Changed
Her Business Forever 8

This Guy Lost $37 Billion By Networking The Wrong Way!
Are You Doing The Same Thing?......................... 11

Are You Focused On This One Secret That Will
Produce The Most Money?................................... 15

Is Your Character For Sale?................................. 19

What Is The Biggest Risk You Have Ever Taken?
What Is It Worth?.. 25

Are You Letting Your Schooling Interfere
With Your Education?.. 30

Do This One Thing And You Will Always
Have Customers... 36

What Is The One Thing That Holds You Back? 40

What Is The Greatest Life Lesson You
Have Ever Learned? 45

What If You Could Turn Today's Problems Into
Tomorrow's Corporations? 51

This Guy Missed The Opportunity Of A Lifetime?
Are You Doing The Same Thing?......................... 55

This Guy Sold $1.8 Billion In Business Because
He Used This One Technique 59

Are You Following the Five Fundamentals Every
Entrepreneur Should Follow? 62

Do This One Thing And Your F.E.A.R.
Will Run And Hide... 67

This One Trait Could Change Your Business Forever 73

You Want To Increase Your Sales? Follow These
Top 10 Sales Fundamentals 77

This One Principle Can Help You Lift The Lid
On Your Success 81

Are You Alice In Wonderland
Or Are You Wile E. Coyote? 86

Your Past Does Not Represent Your Future
If You Will Do This One Thing 89

Introduction

Stories have a way of impacting our emotions. They help us make decisions, feel inspired to take action, or to become a better person. Before the written word, stories were passed down from generation to generation as an oral history. Today stories, parables, analogies help us convey or sell our message to others.

Parables for Profit is an 18-volume series with twenty stories per book to help you move an audience, motivate your teams and to increase your sells. Each series is patterned after the acronym of our M.O.N.E.Y. Matrix™ training modules. The acronym is as follows: M–Mindset, O–Opportunity, N–Networking, E–Entrepreneurship, Y–You (how to better yourself). At the end of each story there is a Call To Action. This is designed to help you build your business or if you are a manager to help your teams increase their revenue.

Each of these stories have been turned into videos that you can access at www.GetMoneyMatrix.com.

———| M.O.N.E.Y. |———

M.O.N.E.Y.

—— MINDSET ——

If You Do This One Thing Each Day— You Will Reach Your Goal

On the wet and frigid banks of Antarctica in October 1911, two teams were striving to be the first people in history to reach the South Pole. Both were the best in their professions and represented the pride of their countries. One was a Norwegian named Roald Amundsen, the other a

MINDSET

Brit named Robert Falcon Scott.

Amundsen knew this goal would not be easily attained. His team would be travelling approximately fourteen hundred miles round-trip in below freezing conditions over uncertain terrain, with no way to communicate with others in case of emergency. He prepared himself, and therefore his team, years in advance by studying first-hand how Eskimos lived in similar conditions, including their clothing and transportation methods. He even over-prepared by bringing enough supplies to last even if they missed all the supply depots along the way. He tried to think of every possible scenario, good or bad, and plan for a solution. Amundsen planned to succeed.

Scott failed to plan. He and his team were ill prepared for the harsh conditions. What little preparation he did was not based on direct research of the environment but rather on his own ideas and conclusions. His team had barely enough supplies to last them between stops at supply depots. While Amundsen's team used Eskimo-proven sled dogs

MINDSET

for transportation, Scott's team used new "motor sledges" which failed within the first few days of the journey. Scott was outraged when his only altitude-measuring thermometer broke; Amundsen had brought four.

Amundsen knew beforehand how far the group should travel each day to reach their goal. He pushed them to continue during bad weather and held them back when they were tempted to go farther than needed under favorable conditions, encouraging them to rest. They stayed consistent. Scott's team would travel till near exhaustion during favorable conditions and stay in their tents and complain during unfavorable ones. They soon fell behind.

Not surprisingly, Amundsen and his team were the first to reach the South Pole. On December 15, 1911, more than a month before Scott's team arrived, they posted the Norwegian flag and then proceeded to home base. They arrived there on January 25th, the precise day he had planned on arriving.

MINDSET

Eight months later, and just ten miles from a supply depot, a British reconnaissance party found the frozen bodies of Scott and two teammates. They had run out of supplies and, being exhausted and depressed, had stopped sometime in mid-March. The whole team perished.

> "I may say that this is the greatest factor—the way in which the expedition is equipped—the way in which every difficulty is foreseen, and precautions taken for meeting or avoiding it. Victory awaits him who has everything in order—luck, people call it. Defeat is certain for him who has neglected to take the necessary precautions in time; this is called bad luck."
>
> — from *The South Pole*, by Roald Amundsen

Call to Action: Mindset

Symbolically, every twenty-mile march has one common characteristic: Clear Performance Markers. Amundsen knew exactly how many miles his team

MINDSET

would march each day. He knew the exact time they would rest. He and his team knew their performance markers.

Today:

Take fifteen minutes and identify what your "Clear Performance Markers" are. How will you track them? Get very clear on what is in your control and what is not in your control. It is not enough to say, 'I want to double my sales this month.' To double your sales, how many phone calls do you need make each day? How many new contacts do you need to have each week? How many social media posts are you going to make? Be very clear on your performance markers and you will reach your goal.

OPPORTUNITY

This Lady Did One Crazy Thing And It Changed Her Business Forever

It was a hot summer afternoon in 1977 in Palo Alto, California. A new "Open" sign hung over the door, yet there were no customers. She wondered to herself, "Have I made a mistake?" She was only twenty years old, no previous business experience, so maybe she erred in getting a bank loan to start

OPPORTUNITY

her new business. This was a new business model, never tried or tested. There was no track record or even a way to know if it would work. But since the customers weren't coming to her, she decided to go to them. She collected her baked goods and headed out to the sidewalk and passed out her fresh cookies under the sign, "Mrs. Fields Chocolate Chippery."

Debbie Fields had a passion, an enthusiasm for her customers and for quality. She was quoted as saying, "Good enough never is." She was constantly told her business idea would not work. The thought back then was that no one would want to buy chocolate chip cookies when you could make them at home.

For 1977, it seemed like an idea destined to fail. However, when you hustle and take your product to the customer, the world will stand up and take notice. This is exactly what happened. Mrs. Fields expanded throughout the 1980s and started franchise opportunities in the 1990s.

With no formal business training, she embraced

OPPORTUNITY

the advancement of technology and made her company a model for efficiency. She was so efficient that her systems were actually used as a model at Harvard Business School. When you are passionate and enthusiastic, you are qualified, regardless of your education or background.

"The important thing is not being afraid to take a chance. Remember, the greatest failure is to not try. Once you find something you love to do, be the best at doing it."

—Debbie Fields

Call to Action: Opportunity

In the next five minutes do the one thing you have been afraid to do for your business. Debbie Fields could have stayed in the comfort of her air-conditioned store, but instead she took her product to the streets. Make that one phone call, the one hello, the one email or text or social media post to your potential customer. If you will do this activity, you will see your fear subside and your sales increase.

NETWORKING

**This Guy Lost $37 Billion
By Networking The Wrong Way!
Are You Doing
The Same Thing?**

Early in Walt Disney's career, he lost his prized character, Oswald the Rabbit, to Charlie Mintz who basically took it from him through clever contracts. It had been Disney's first commercial success. On a train ride back to California, Disney came up with

NETWORKING

a new character called Mortimer Mouse. His wife said the name was not cute enough and suggested he change it to Mickey Mouse.

As Walt and his brother Roy were building Disney Studios, they created many partnerships to expand their business. After the failure with Mintz, they turned to New York film distributor Pat Powers to put their cartoons into movie houses across America. Walt traveled back to New York to find out why their payments from Powers kept getting smaller, even though the brothers were turning out more cartoons. Powers had secretly been holding back money and not paying them so that he could crush Walt and Roy and take Mickey Mouse from them.

Powers offered Walt a job to come work for him at $2,500 a week, which is $130,000 a year. This was a lot of money back then considering the President of the United States was only making $75,000 a year in 1930. Powers didn't understand Walt's resolve. Walt only wanted the money so that he could run his own shop. He didn't have

NETWORKING

the desire to ever work for anybody else.

But Walt's spirit would be crushed when his long-time friend, business partner, and animator, Ub Iwerks, networked behind Walt's back with Powers and signed a secret deal to have Powers fund Iwerks' own studio. Iwerks would be making three times what he was making at Disney. The problem was that it started a domino effect with other talented artists, such as composer Carl Stalling, also networking behind Walt's back because they knew that the Disney studio was destined to fail.

Walt was so disheartened and saddened by Iwerks' decision that it nearly crushed him. Iwerks owned 20 percent of the Disney Company, which he ended up selling back to Walt and Roy for $2,920. Today, a 20 percent stake in The Walt Disney Company is worth over $37 billion.

Even though Walt and Roy were on the verge of closing their studio after most of the talent left and joined Iwerks Studio, the Disney brothers reached deep into their network to find people who wanted

NETWORKING

to fill the positions now left vacant. As history has proven, the Disney studio bounced back and has dominated the animation scene ever since. Iwerks was not as lucky. Within six years, his studio went out of business, and by 1940, he was working again at Disney animation but this time as an employee and not an owner.

Call to Action: Networking

Are you networking like Mintz, Powers, and Iwerks, or do you network like Walt Disney? Are you open in your communications, or are you secretly doing backhanded deals? Take fifteen minutes today and identify one individual you want to get to know better. Reach out to them via text, email, phone, or social media, and set up an appointment.

Remember to create value first. Solve their business problem before you present your idea or business opportunity to them. Remember, people do not care how much you know until they know how much you care.

ENTREPRENEURSHIP

**Are You Focused On
This One Secret
That Will Produce
The Most Money?**

Only an entrepreneur has the ability to leverage themselves through sales, products, distributors, and marketing systems. There will be many times when you feel it is an uphill battle. Hang in there, it is worth it.

ENTREPRENEURSHIP

Consider the following entrepreneurs:

Fred Smith, the founder of FedEx, was mocked by his college professor when he submitted his idea of overnight package delivery. After investing $22 million for planes, trucks, and distribution channels, they only received eighteen packages the first day.

J.K. Rowling's first publication run of Harry Potter and the Sorcerer's Stone was only for fifteen hundred copies. No one anticipated the worldwide success of her little story of a wizard and his friends.

Readers Digest was rejected by every major publisher of its time.

Colonel Sanders did not find financial success for his special recipe for chicken until he was seventy-six. He ended up selling Kentucky Fried Chicken for $17 million.

When Alexander Bell invented the telephone, he offered the rights to Western Union for $100,000. The offer was disdainfully rejected with the pronouncement, "What use could this company make

ENTREPRENEURSHIP

of an electrical toy."

Joyce Hall, founder of Hallmark, received a phone call that his entire inventory had been destroyed in a fire. He did not have enough insurance to cover his debts or to reorder more inventory. Within twenty-four hours, he and his brother secured their own printing press and started making their own designs and cards.

Ole Kirk Christiansen was losing so much money that he turned to his family for financial help. They loaned him the money on one condition: "No more making toys." He borrowed the money but didn't listen to their advice. He eventually renamed his company LEGO.

"I've missed more than 9,000 shots in my career. I've lost almost 300 games. Twenty-six times I've been trusted to take the game's winning shot and missed. I've failed over and over and over again in my life and that's why I succeed."

—Michael Jordan, NBA Hall of Famer.

Every entrepreneur has days when they feel they have failed, and they don't believe they can make

ENTREPRENEURSHIP

it one more day. Like all the greats listed above, the only way they turned their businesses and careers around was to focus on their IPAs (their Income Producing Activities). This singular focus will catapult you from where you are to where you want to be financially.

Call to Action: Entrepreneurship

Today:

What are your IPAs (Income Producing Activities)? They might be phone calls, demonstrations, speaking engagements, knocking doors, handing out flyers, networking, referrals, or promoting your next event. Identify your best IPAs and spend the next eight hours focused only those activities.

YOU

Is Your Character For Sale?

James' first entrepreneurial experience was owning the butcher shop in his hometown. To get the business of the local hotel, he was required to buy a bottle of liquor for the head cook each week. James did not smoke or drink, so he refused to pay the bribe to do business with the hotel. Consequently, his butcher business failed. Later he would say, "I lost everything that I had, but I learned never to compromise." By sticking to his morals, he opened another store called the "Golden Rule." Eventually, James Cash Penney changed the name of the store to J.C. Penney.

William struggled in school. After being kicked out of school for the third time, his father made him work ten hours a day in the family business. Over time, he got married and moved out on his own. He started his entrepreneur experience by selling umbrellas, newspapers, and gum. It wasn't until he was thirty-two years old that he had any success with chewing gum. Six years later, his competitors tried to put him out of business because he would not join an illegal, price-fixing cartel with them. When William Wrigley Jr. was forty-six years old, there was a serious economic depression that put most people out of business, and which almost forced him into bankruptcy. Due to his character and reputation, he could secure a business loan for $250,000, almost twice his annual sales revenue. By putting the money into a national advertising campaign, within one year his

YOU

sales revenue went from $170,000 to $3 million. How to Strengthen Your Character:

Keep Your Word: In Dr. Seuss's book, Horton Hatches the Egg, Horton the Elephant agrees to sit on Lazy Mayzie's egg in her nest. Sweet Lazy Mayzie disappears and does not return even though she promises she will. As the other animals see Horton sitting in a tree, they begin to mock him. His reply should be put up as an anthem in every business. He said, "I meant what I said and I said what I meant; an elephant is faithful 100 percent." You should always endeavor to keep your word at all cost.

Honor Your Time: Imagine that there is a bank that credits your account each morning with $86,400, carries over no balance from day to day, allows you to keep no cash balance, and every evening cancels whatever part of the amount that you had failed to use during the day. What would you do? Draw out every cent, of course! Well, everyone has such a bank. Its name is time. Every morning, it credits you with 86,400 seconds. Whatever you have not used for a good purpose is written off as a loss each night. It carries over no balance. It allows no overdraft. The clock is running. Make the most of today.

Call to Action: You

Today:

Take fifteen minutes and journal about a time you had a tough decision to make and how your character was tested. Reflect on the actions you took. Good and bad habits are formed in our daily routine. As you identify your past successes in making difficult choices, you will be more like to make character driven decisions in the future.

---| M.O.N.E.Y. |---

SERIES

2

M.O.N.E.Y.

| MINDSET |

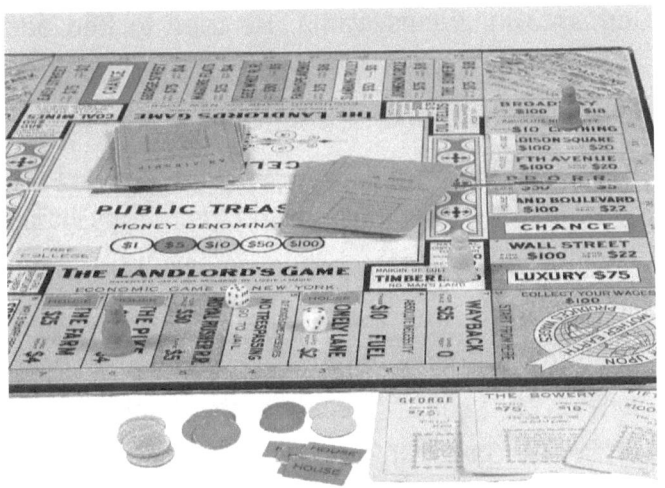

What Is The Biggest Risk You Have Ever Taken? What Is It Worth?

Have you ever been fired? Being fired can be the most depressing experiences of your career. During the height of the Great Depression, Charles Darrow was fired from his job. He was barely able to make ends meet, and along with his pregnant wife and small child, he lived in a rundown, old house in

MINDSET

Germantown, Pennsylvania. He tried to find odd jobs mowing lawns or doing manual labor, but times were hard and he competed with other unemployed men for the simplest of jobs. To pass the time in the evenings, he and his friends would play a homemade game where you would buy and sell real estate.

For the previous thirty years, there had been many such games, including the original, *The Landlord's Game*, invented by Elizabeth (Lizzie) Maggie in 1904. She patented the board game that same year, and in 1910 and 1924 she presented the game to George Parker, of Parker Brothers, who turned her down. The game that Darrow played in 1933 was a knockoff version of Lizzie's. He became so enamored of the game that he started making his own version using linoleum flooring for the board. He added a few new twists and named the properties after locations in his home town.

On May 31, 1934, Darrow pitched his version to Milton Bradley, and he was quickly rejected. Undaunted, he took it to Parker Brothers, who on

---- MINDSET ----

October 19, 1934 not only turned it down but also wrote a personal note explaining the 52 reasons why this game was not a good idea, as well as listing in great detail why they thought that it would never sell in that consumer market. Here is where history was made because Darrow could have given up like Lizzie had, and he could have just assumed that it wasn't going to sell. He had 52 reasons from the "experts" outlining why his version was not a marketable idea.

Competition was rampant among others who were also making their own versions of the game. It isn't difficult to imagine the conversation he must have had with his wife, who by now had two small children, when he told her he wanted to be an entrepreneur. Given his situation—unemployed during the Great Depression, a small young family to take care of, manufacturing competitors, and the experts 'proof' of failure—who would think his little board game "Monopoly" would ever do well?

At the height of the worst economical depression, when men and women were standing in breadlines, Darrow borrowed $5,000 from family and friends to produce Monopoly Board Games. Without a retail location or orders from other stores, he decided to be proactive and started selling his games on street corners. As people played it and shared it with their friends, orders started coming in from around the country.

When the Parker Brothers (George and Charles) got wind of his surprise success, they offered to buy his company. He graciously turned them down, but confident after his success in selling his product, he countered and offered them a licensing deal. Parker Brothers quickly signed a royalty agreement that gave Darrow a percentage of each Monopoly game sold for decades. To eliminate competition, Parker Brothers bought up each competitor including Lizzie Maggie's game that they bought for $500 (with no royalties).

What was the primary difference between Charles Darrow and Lizzie Maggie and the other competitors? MINDSET! Each of them sold out for a one-time payment. Only Darrow was paid a royalty

MINDSET

on each product which then turned him into a multi-millionaire.

Determination, drive, fearlessness, innovation, and inspiration all come from having a positive mindset. When you have the courage to press forward when the "experts" say it is impossible, then you have the ability to create your own future.

Call to Action: Mindset

Imagine for a second you have a positive mindset. Breathe it in and embrace it. Close your eyes if you need to. If you were the smartest person in the world, what is the one thing you would do for your business today? No Fear–No Excuses. Do not second guess your impression. Listen to that positive voice in your head. Quickly write down your answer, and put all your energy into accomplishing it in the next two hours. If you do this, you, like Darrow, will see your business dramatically improve.

OPPORTUNITY

Are You Letting Your Schooling Interfere With Your Education?

According to the U.S. Department of Education, almost 10 percent of high school students drop out. That 10 percent is then considered not qualified for 90 percent of the jobs offered in the United States. These dropouts will make, on average, $260,000 less than a high school graduate and

OPPORTUNITY

roughly $1,000,000 less than a college graduate over their lifetime. With these staggering statistics, here is a list of forty high school and college dropouts who have created their own opportunities regardless of their limited education:

- Dov Charney, founder of American Apparel
- Amadeo Giannini, founder of Bank of America
- Ben Cohen, founder of Ben & Jerry's Homemade Ice Cream
- William Boeing, founder of The Boeing Company
- Asa Candler, founder of The Coca Cola Company
- Harry Cohen, founder of Columbia Pictures Industries, Inc.
- Russell Simmons, founder of Def Jam Recordings
- Michael Dell, founder of Dell Inc.
- Tom Monaghan, founder of Domino's Pizza L.L.C.
- Charles Dow, founder of Dow Jones & Company, Inc.

OPPORTUNITY

- David Geffen and Steven Spielberg, co-founders of DreamWorks SKG
- Florence Graham, founder of Elizabeth Arden, Inc.
- Henry Ford, founder of Ford Motor Company
- Mark Zuckerberg, founder of Facebook
- King Gillette, founder of The Gillette Company
- Milton Hershey, founder of The Hershey Company
- Kemmons Wilson, founder of Holiday Inn
- Soichiro Honda, founder of Honda Automotive
- David Neeleman, founder of JetBlue Airways
- Jimmy Dean, founder of Jimmy Dean Foods
- Colonel Sanders, founder of Kentucky Fried Chicken
- Marcus Loew, founder of Loews Theatres
- William Lear, founder of Lear Jets
- Ole Kirk Christian, founder of Lego
- Frank Mars, founder of Mars Candies
- Ruth Handler, founder of Mattel Corp
- Ray Kroc, founder of McDonald's Corporation

OPPORTUNITY

- Bill Gates, founder of Microsoft Corporation
- Berry Gordy, founder of Motown Records
- David Sarnoff, founder of NBC
- Larry Ellison, founder of Oracle
- Patrick Frawley, founder of Paper Mate Pens
- Ralph Lauren, founder of Polo and the Ralph Lauren Corporation
- James Gamble, founder of Proctor & Gamble
- Jann Wenner, founder of Rolling Stone Magazine
- Frederick Royce, founder of Rolls-Royce Limited
- Vidal Sassoon, founder of Vidal Sassoon Hair Products
- Sir Richard Branson, founder of Virgin Enterprises, Ltd.
- Dave Thomas, founder of Wendy's International, Inc.
- John Mackey, founder of Whole Foods Market

OPPORTUNITY

The Top 5 Ways to Create Opportunities:

Start Close to Home: Define your strengths, talents, and expertise. Create a niche for yourself.

Obey the Law of Reciprocity: You have to give to receive. Reach out to other people and see how you can help them. As you give service, you will discover available opportunities.

Create a Plan: If you fail to plan, then you plan to fail. What is your plan? Where do you want to be in the next one, five, and ten years?

Be Flexible: Even though you have a plan, you should remain flexible. If you take an opportunity that is not 100 percent what you want, then it may lead to a better opportunity down the road.

Keep Your Eyes Open: Even if your current opportunities are thriving, what can you do to make your current opportunity more profitable?

> "Don't wait for extraordinary opportunities. Seize common occasions and make them great. Weak men wait for opportunities; strong men make them."
>
> —Orison Swett Marden

OPPORTUNITY

Call to Action: Opportunities

Today:

Take the next ten minutes and identify the top five benefits you receive from your business. How can you use those to your advantage when you are selling what you do? If you know why you love what you do other people will respond to your enthusiasm. If you do this activity you will see an increase in appreciation for your current opportunities which will become contagious as you share it with others.

NETWORKING

**Do This One Thing
And You Will Always
Have Customers**

The roar of the V12 engine from Eddie Van Halen's Lamborghini filled the streets of Los Angeles as he pulled into Claudio Zampolli's shop. Eddie had noticed a cherry red Ferrari 512 Boxer on display in the showroom. Zampolli, the shop owner, told him it belonged to Sammy Hagar and asked Eddie if

NETWORKING

he wanted to meet him. The band Van Halen had just separated ways with their lead singer, David Lee Roth, and was in need of a new front man. So, Eddie called Hagar from the shop phone.

The two knew each other slightly. Eddie was not the type of man to waste time with small talk, so he asked Hagar if he wanted to be in Van Halen and do a record together. Hagar had never really liked the group. Though he liked Eddie's guitar playing, he thought Roth's raunchy, larger-than-life persona was phony and repetitive. Hagar didn't want to be in someone else's band, but Eddie persuaded him to just come for a few days.

Hagar flew to L.A. for a meeting with the Van Halen brothers, and the three men went to Eddie's garage and started jamming. When the brothers started playing a riff on guitar and drums, Hagar would make up the lyrics. They wrote two songs right there on the spot. The next morning, Hagar called and said, "I'm in."

Prior to Hagar, the band Van Halen had never had a #1 album. Each of the four albums featuring

NETWORKING

Sammy Hagar went straight to #1 and sold millions of copies. With their newfound wealth from each of their albums, where do you think that they went to buy their next cars? They went to Claudio Zampolli.

When you network, you do not have to have an immediate benefit. Networking is not going to a business meeting and pitching business cards to everyone you see. Networking is about solving problems for people; it is not about promoting yourself. The fastest way to promote yourself is to solve someone else's problem. They will forever remember you, and they will typically refer you to their inner circle.

Top 5 Ways to Network:

Create Value for Others First: What are their needs and how can you solve them?

Branch Out: Join a networking club. There are many in almost every city.

Differentiate Yourself: Be the best at something. What is your expertise?

Follow Up: Regularly reach out to your network,

and see what you can do to add value to their business.

Be Concise: Networking goes both ways. Know what you need so that when someone asks you, "What do you need?" you have an answer. The worst thing that you can say is "I am fine." What that means is that they have no value to offer you.

Call to Action: Networking

Today:

Call one person in your network, and invest fifteen minutes into helping them solve one of their problems. See if there is anyone in your network that you can introduce them to in order to help them. As you make deposits into other people's accounts, when you are in need you will be able to make a withdrawal. Remember, people are like bank accounts: If you make more deposits than withdrawals, you will become rich in terms of money and friends.

ENTREPRENEURSHIP

What Is The One Thing That Holds You Back?

Rowland opened his first store in Boston the same year he was married. Within a short time, he and his new bride had to close their doors as they did not know how to run a retail business. Undaunted, he quickly opened another store, which lasted only two years. At the age of twenty-seven, he went west to California to try his luck on a third store.

ENTREPRENEURSHIP

He assumed a new location would remedy his situation. But within a year, this store also failed, and he packed his bags and moved back home. He was discouraged, but he refocused and set up a fourth store in Haverhill, Massachusetts; this went bankrupt within two years.

By the time he was thirty-six he was considered a massive failure by the world's standards. However, he thought differently from others, and he was determined to make his mark in business. By learning from his many mistakes, he consulted experts on how to properly handle inventory, financing, shipping, employee training, and store layout. In 1858, Rowland Macy opened his fifth store in Herald Square in New York City and it became the world's largest department store; and it is still the world's largest department store, over 156 years later.

What was the difference between the first four failures and the enormous success of his fifth store? He finally learned the Business Behind the Business. Part of succeeding is learning what does not work.

ENTREPRENEURSHIP

Examples of Entrepreneurs Who Learned the Business Behind the Business:

Ole Kirk Christiansen was losing so much money in his business that he turned to his family for financial help. They loaned him the money on one condition: "no more making toys." He ended up borrowing the money but kept making toys. He eventually changed the name of the company to LEGO.

Soichiro Honda was turned down by Toyota Motor Corporation during a job interview for an engineer position. He continued to be jobless until his neighbors started buying his "homemade scooters." Subsequently, he started his own company, the Honda Motor Company. Today, the company has grown to become the world's largest motorcycle manufacturer, and his automotive company is more profitable than rival automakers, GM and Chrysler.

Akio Morita, the founder of Sony Corporation, had a failure for a first product, an electric rice cooker. He only sold 100 cookers because they burned the rice rather than cooking it. Today, Sony

ENTREPRENEURSHIP

generates $66 billion in revenue, and it is ranked as one of the world's largest electronic companies.

John Grisham's first novel was rejected by sixteen agents and twelve publishing houses. Despite these rejections, he continued writing until he became best known as a novelist specializing in the genre of legal thrillers. The media has called him one of the best authors alive in the 21st century.

Call to Action: Entrepreneurship

Today:

Take five minutes and identify the one thing that is holding you back in business. Most likely someone somewhere has found the solution to your exact problem. Take the next thirty minutes and research a solution to your problem. Search online, consult with a trusted business advisor, or ask someone higher up in your company for the answer. We don't know what we don't know, but if we let go of our pride and embarrassment we find solutions very rapidly. Imagine what Mr. Macy's first four businesses would have been like if he would have asked for help. Be like other successful entrepreneurs who sought the missing information they needed to reach their next level.

--- YOU ---

What Is The Greatest Life Lesson You Have Ever Learned?

At every high school or college graduation, someone gives a commencement speech. The definition of commencement means "a beginning or a new start." If you were to write a commencement speech for your life right now what would you say? If one part of your life was coming to a completion

YOU

and you were starting new, what would you tell yourself?

Here are excerpts from two phenomenal commencement speeches to give you some ideas:

Jim Carrey—Commencement speech, Maharishi University of Management, 2014:

"So many of us choose our path out of fear disguised as practicality. What we really want seems impossibly out of reach and ridiculous to expect, so we never dare to ask the universe for it. I'm saying, I'm the proof that you can ask the universe for it—please! And if it doesn't happen for you right away, it's only because the universe is so busy fulfilling my order. It's party size!

My father could have been a great comedian, but he didn't believe that was possible for him, and so he made a conservative choice. Instead, he got a safe job as an accountant, and when I was twelve-years old, he was let go from that safe job and our family had to do whatever we could to survive. I learned many great lessons from my father, not the least of which was that you can fail at what

YOU

you don't want, so you might as well take a chance on doing what you love."

Steve Jobs — Commencement speech, Stanford University, 2005:

"Sometimes life is going to hit you in the head with a brick. Don't lose faith. I am convinced the only thing that kept me going was that I loved what I did. Your work is going to fill a large part of your life and the only way to be truly satisfied is to do what you believe to be great work. And the only way to do great work is to love what you do. When I was seventeen, I read a quote that went something like: "If you live each day as if it was your last, someday you'll most certainly be right." It made an impression on me, and since then, for the past thirty-three years, I have looked in the mirror every morning and asked myself: "If today were the last day of my life, would I want to do what I am about to do today?" And whenever the answer has been "No" for too many days in a row, I know I need to change something. Stay Hungry. Stay Foolish. And I have always wished that for myself. And now, as

| YOU |

you graduate to begin anew, I wish that for you."

And remember, by 2005 Apple had not yet launched the iPhone, iPad, iPod Touch, Apple TV, or the MacBook. Steve Jobs is an incredible example of Staying Hungry & Staying Foolish.

Call to Action: You

Today:

Take thirty minutes and write your commencement speech in three hundred words. It is the equivalent of a twelve-line paragraph. What advice would you give to yourself? What would you acknowledge about your past? What experiences would you want to remember? When you are done post it on the wall in your office as a constant reminder of who you are and what you believe the future holds.

---| M.O.N.E.Y. |---

3

M.O.N.E.Y.

--- MINDSET ---

What If You Could Turn Today's Problems Into Tomorrow's Corporations?

When Conrad was growing up, he wanted to be like his dad, a successful entrepreneur who owned many of the businesses in their small town. However, when his father found him sleeping in past 7:00 a.m. one day, he labeled him as a "lazy oaf who would never amount to anything." But, Conrad refused to believe this label applied to him; he became very driven with a winning mindset

MINDSET

and a disciplined work ethic. He threw himself into his education and entered politics after graduation winning a seat in the state legislature of New Mexico. After serving two years in politics, he persuaded his father to open a bank with him. He started as a teller and within a couple of years worked his way up to become bank president. Upon becoming the bank president, Conrad tried to buy the bank from his father but he refused.

So Conrad decided to break out on his own and looked for a different bank to buy. He had enough connections in the industry to borrow the money, plus, he had saved some money on his own. After two barely missed opportunities to buy a small bank, he went to Cisco, Texas, where a banker was selling one. Conrad did not negotiate the price because he had already been out-bid twice before. The seller took Conrad's speedy offer as an impression that he might be selling it for too little so he quickly raised the price, which frustrated Conrad. He went to the local hotel to find a room. Upon watching the bustling lobby, where there were more people than

MINDSET

rooms, he asked the owner about his business. The owner acknowledged his business was healthy, but what he really wanted to do was to try his hand in the oil business. After talking for a little while and checking the hotel's financials, Conrad offered to buy it. By the end of the day, Conrad Hilton was the proud owner of his first hotel.

He could have focused on the label his dad had put upon him. He could have given up when he did not have the opportunity to buy the bank from his father. However, even though he was out to buy a bank, he had the right mindset to recognize a good opportunity when he saw one. When the opportunity arose, he was prepared to meet the challenge. Today's problems can be tomorrow's corporations.

Having a winning mindset means you are flexible. At the end of the day, Hilton didn't necessarily want to be a banker. He wanted to be an entrepreneur. With his winning mindset, he was able to take advantage of the opportunity right in front of him.

— MINDSET —

Call to Action: Mindset

Today:

Take the next ten minutes and list the opportunities in front of you right now. With a winning mindset, which opportunities do you need to fully engage in and which ones do you need to walk away from? If you do this activity, it will increase your resolve to succeed and strengthen your business.

OPPORTUNITY

This Guy Missed The Opportunity Of A Lifetime?
Are You Doing The Same Thing?

Two friends watched as jackrabbits scattered before them on the dirt road; they were driving out past the city limits among open fields spotted with horses and orchards. Walter pulled the car over, and he vividly described what he was going to build on this desolate land to his friend, Arthur.

OPPORTUNITY

He wanted to convince his friend to buy all the surrounding acreage. Walter told Arthur, "I can handle the main project myself. It will take all my money, but I want you to have the first chance at this surrounding acreage, because in the next year it will double in value." Arthur looked around and thought to himself, "Who in the world is going to drive 25 miles for this crazy project? His dream has gotten the best of his common sense." Arthur gave Walter all the excuses a good friend could give while trying not to squash his dreams. And though Walter continued to implore him to buy the remaining land, Arthur would not concede. He gave a few more excuses about how money was a little tight, and that it was not the best time to invest, and said that he would think about it. Walter cautioned, "Later on will be too late. You had better move on it right now."

But in the end, Art Linkletter failed to see the vision of his close friend Walt Disney. One year later, on July 18, 1955, Art was the master of ceremonies when Walt opened Disneyland. Art had missed out on the opportunity of a lifetime

OPPORTUNITY

by failing to purchase the land surrounding one of today's most well-known amusement parks. Walt's mind had been set on building Disneyland. He even cashed in his life insurance policy to raise the necessary funds to build his dream. Art's mindset, however, was that the opportunity was too risky. He justified this feeling by claiming money was too tight. Frankly, he didn't feel Walt's vision would work, and so he passed on the opportunity. Within eight weeks of it opening, Disneyland greeted its one millionth visitor.

In 1954, the same year Walt Disney was building his dream, the Fujishige family had a different mindset; they envisioned what the land around it could become. They purchased fifty-six acres of strawberry fields across the street from Disneyland for $10,000. In the late 1990's, the Disney Corporation paid the family just under $100 million for the land.

An opportunity is an opportunity regardless of whether friends or strangers believe in it. At some point, you will likely have friends who will pass on opportunities that you present. Too often, the value

OPPORTUNITY

we put on an opportunity is directly related to the approval of our inner circle of friends and family. When Walt was building Disneyland, everyone, including his brother and business partner Roy, did not believe in his concept for a family theme park. Over time, both his friends as well as complete strangers saw his vision, and many bought into his opportunity.

Opportunities come and go, but a person with the right mindset has the potential to create an opportunity out of any situation.

Call to Action: Opportunity

Today:

Take the next ten minutes and list the value of your opportunities. What was the value of Disneyland for Walt? How valuable are your current opportunities to you? What will they be worth one year, five years, and ten years from now? If you do this activity, you will have the energy to keep promoting and sharing your opportunities with others which will only increase the value of your business over time.

NETWORKING

This Guy Sold $1.8 Billion In Business Because He Used This One Technique

Before Chris Cortazzo became the #1 Real Estate Agent in Malibu, and before he sold $1.8 billion in real estate transactions, he was an assistant to celebrity photographer Herb Ritts. On one of Herb's shoots in Malibu, he was with actor Richard Gere. Cortazzo overheard Gere talking about how much

NETWORKING

he loved this certain house nearby. Chris said, "I just kayaked by it three days ago, and it is for sale for $5 million." Later that week, Gere, his business manager, and Chris all met at the house, and Richard fell in love with it. He bought the home and launched Chris' real estate career.

Though Cortazzo was from Malibu, and was passionate about the area, this alone was not enough. He needed contacts, clients, potential sellers, and buyers. At first, these relationships came through his network with Herb Ritts. Through these relationships, people would ask him, "Since you are from Malibu, where should I buy a house?" He was solving problems for people. And these people started referring their friends and business partners to Cortazzo.

Where would Cortazzo be without his relationship with Ritts? Most likely, he would be a starving, new, real estate agent who would never have gone on to sell $1.8 billion in transactions. Relationships are absolutely crucial to success. However, you have to add value to your network through selfless service

NETWORKING

and a disciplined work ethic.

Networking is defined as "a supportive system of sharing information and services among individuals and groups that have a common interest." Networking is NOT about self-promotion, talking about your accomplishments, making others feel small, or being the only person in the room with the right idea.

Call to Action: Networking

Today:

Take the next ten minutes and identify a business associate you have not talked to in the last thirty days. Give them a call and see how you can serve them or help them in any way. Remember, Cortazzo built a $1.8 billion sales empire simply by solving other people's problems first. If you will do this on a continual basis you will find your calendar will fill up very quickly with referrals.

ENTREPRENEURSHIP

**Are You Following
the Five Fundamentals
Every Entrepreneur
Should Follow?**

To thrive in today's new economy you can't conform or copy. To be a successful entrepreneur, you have to be different. Here are five things successful entrepreneurs do to help them stand out.

ENTREPRENEURSHIP

1. They model, not copy.

When you're frustrated with the lack of progress and income in your business, you naturally look to those who are successful. You think if you copy what they're doing, you could get the results they're getting. Unfortunately, it doesn't work that way.

When you're the carbon copy of someone else, people will do business with the original person, not you. Model those systems that work and use successful frameworks. Learn from the strategies that make them successful, but do it in a way that's unique to you and your business.

2. They're clear about who their customer is.

Successful entrepreneurs serve a specific target market. Think of Niches to Riches. They realize that you can't reach everyone, and if you try, your efforts will be ineffective and scattered. To grow your business, you have to spend your time and resources in the places that will get you the best results.

Chasing people who will probably never buy from you is not a great use of your time. Time is money for entrepreneurs. Wasting it in the places unlikely to generate income is not what helps you become successful.

3. They don't rely too heavily on any one strategy.
Social media has been great for businesses, but it has become the crutch for too many entrepreneurs. Successful entrepreneurs have a very diverse strategy that doesn't rely too heavily on any one thing. They realize that at any time, what used to work might not any more. They leave room to pivot.

A case in point, when Google and Facebook changed their searching algorithms it put some entrepreneurs out of business because they were to heavily invested in this one strategy. The smart entrepreneurs moved on to Plan B.

4. They keep it simple.
We live in a time when information is readily available. Every day, we listen to podcasts, watch videos, and read blogs that give us amazing strategies to grow our business. The problem comes in the

form of information overload.

We get stuck because we get confused about what we should be working on right now and what will lead to the best results. Successful entrepreneurs firmly believe in the speed of implementation. How fast can you take a good idea and create a product or service from that idea?

Successful entrepreneurs realize that seeking perfection is a curse. Instead, they get their idea to market and improve upon it through customer feedback. They keep it simple by learning, then implementing.

5. They don't let self-limiting beliefs stunt their business.

At some point in their journey, every successful entrepreneur has struggled with self-limiting beliefs. You will too. These beliefs are things that you're telling yourself that hinder the actions you take in your business. The beliefs could be:

Your content isn't good enough.

You can't raise your prices.

ENTREPRENEURSHIP

There's too much competition.
You don't have enough credentials.
You don't have enough resources.

Successful entrepreneurs have beaten these self-limiting beliefs and keep them from creeping back into their mind. If you're going to be successful in anything, it starts in your mind.

Call to Action: Entrepreneurship

Today:

Take the next fifteen minutes and interview three past customers/clients and find out why they chose to work with you. If you do this you may find a pattern that will reveal your ideal customer and how to find more of them.

| YOU |

**Do This One Thing
And Your F.E.A.R.
Will Run And Hide**

When is the last time you felt fear? There are two types of fear. First, there is self-preservation fear that you feel when you are trying to preserve your life. This fear leads directly to a "fight or flight" response. Animals also experience this type of fear. When a lion chases a gazelle across the

YOU

African plains, that gazelle feels a "fight or flight" type of fear. We as humans feel the same when it comes to survival.

However, that is not the fear that holds us back in our business. The type of fear that holds us back from making calls, fills our mind with doubt, or makes us worry about money, is best summed up in the acronym of F.E.A.R.: False Evidence Appearing Real. This fear is not real. It seems real, and it holds us back, but it has not happened yet. To illustrate this point, let's say you're hiking in the hills, and as you round a corner, you suddenly see a huge rattlesnake in the middle of the trail with his rattle shaking and his fangs exposed. What would you be afraid he would do? You would probably be afraid he would bite you, right? Now let's say you were to take a step back and WHAM! He bites you in the leg. Now what are you afraid is going to happen? You are probably afraid you are going to die; you are no longer afraid he is going to bite you. Fear is always a potential event. You cannot feel fear in the moment. You can feel the effects of fear, but you

YOU

cannot actually feel the fear. After the snake bites you, you are no longer afraid of him biting you. Your fear moves onto the next potential problem, the fear of death. Fear is always a potential event. Mark Twain said it best when he said, "I've experienced many terrible things in my life, a few of which actually happened."

For you to overcome F.E.A.R., you must have a dream bigger than it. The only thing F.E.A.R. is afraid of is something larger than itself. You must have an internal dream so ridiculously enormous that your F.E.A.R. runs and hides. "Courage is not the absence of fear, but rather the judgment that something else is more important than fear," said Ambrose Redmoon. Mark Twain said, "Courage is resistance to fear; mastery of fear-not absence of fear."

Just for fun, here are few other acronyms of F.E.A.R. that may give you some insight. The last one is the most important.

- False Evidence Appearing Real
- Forget Everything And Run
- Forever Evading All Riches

| YOU |

- Future Events Appearing Real
- Faith Escapes, Anguish Returns
- False Expectations Are Realized
- Fantasized Expectations About Reality
- Face Everything And Resolve
- F.E.A.R.—Fearless Entrepreneur Achieving Results

Call to Action: You

Today:

Take the next fifteen minutes and identify a fear you have about your business. For example, it could be the fear of rejection, the fear of running out of money, or the fear of being misunderstood. Now, what is a clear, defined dream bigger than that fear? For example, it could be being the top sales person in your company, paying cash for your next car, or engaging multiple people in your business. Remember, what you focus on you feel. If you will do this activity and create a dream bigger than your fear, your fear will be forced to run and hide.

| M.O.N.E.Y. |

SERIES

4

M.O.N.E.Y.

---- MINDSET ----

**This One Trait
Could Change
Your Business Forever**

In 1883, an engineer named John Roebling was inspired by an idea to build a spectacular bridge connecting New York with Long Island. However, bridge building experts throughout the world thought that it was an impossible feat and told Roebling to forget

MINDSET

the idea. It just could not be done. It was not practical. It had never been done before.

Roebling could not ignore the vision he had in his mind of this bridge. He managed to convince his son Washington, an up and coming engineer, that the bridge could in fact be built. Working together for the first time, the father and son hired their crew and began to build their dream bridge.

The project started well, but when it was only a few months underway, a tragic accident on the site took the life of John Roebling. His son Washington was injured and left with brain damage, resulting in him being unable to walk, talk, or even move.

Comments of "We told them so," "Crazy men and their crazy dreams," and "It's foolish to chase wild visions" were spread around and even published in the papers. People believed the project should be scrapped because no one believed it could be built.

As Washington lay on his bed in his hospital room, sunlight streamed through the windows, and a gentle breeze blew the flimsy white curtains apart;

MINDSET

he was able to see the sky and the tops of the trees outside for just a moment. It seemed that there was a message for him not to give up. Suddenly an idea hit him. All he could do was move one finger, and he decided to make the best use of it.

By moving his finger, he slowly developed a code of communication with his wife. He touched his wife's arm, instructing her to call all the engineers. Then, he used the same method of tapping her arm to tell the engineers what to do. The project was under way again.

For thirteen years, Washington tapped out his instructions with his finger on his wife's arm until the bridge was finally completed. Today, the spectacular Brooklyn Bridge stands in all its glory, a tribute to a man's indomitable spirit and a woman's ability to not be defeated by their circumstances.

Never give up on your passion and dreams. There are future generations who need what you are building right now. You are the only one who can deliver your special talents and traits.

What allowed the Roeblings to finish this

insurmountable problem? It was their mindset to win and conquer their fear and challenges. Whether you are building a bridge or your business, it is the same. It will take everything you have. Keep your vision in sight. Never lose focus on what you want to achieve.

Call to Action: Mindset

Today:

Take the next ten minutes and create a 3"x5" picture (drawing, photograph, image, etc) of exactly what you want to achieve in the next six months. Put it in a frame and place it on your desk so that you do not lose sight of your target. Remember, you cannot hit a target you cannot see. If you will do this you will have a constant reminder of the direction you need to go.

OPPORTUNITY

You Want To Increase Your Sales? Follow These Top 10 Sales Fundamentals

Be a Product of The Product:
If you are not sold on your own product or service, it will be an uphill battle to sell someone else. Your lack of conviction will be completely transparent. Be clear and direct: When selling, do not use complicated diction. Pride yourself instead on being

OPPORTUNITY

able to explain the concept as quickly, clearly, and simply as possible. This is important because the biggest problem in sales is client confusion. Confusion does not lead to a Yes.

Know your client:
Make sure to research your potential clients, know their challenges and their needs. One size hardly ever fits all. You look much stronger if you care about the business enough to invest in the research.

It's all about the presentation:
Practice it, memorize it, and be prepared to shift your emphasis based on how the energy changes when you give the presentation.

Be passionate and exciting: Most presentations are BORING! So create a show and make it exciting! Excitement is contagious.

If you don't know the answer, do not guess: People will ask you tough questions, and you may not always know the answer. The person asking you may be

OPPORTUNITY

testing you, knowing the answer full well. Know what you are talking about. Practice, Practice, Practice.

Answer questions directly and clearly:
If you are asked a question and you give a "politician's answer"—in other words, if you don't directly answer the question—your credibility will decline, and you will hurt your chances of making the sale.

You can always be better:
Sales is an art, not a science. This means it's never perfect and can always improve.

Dress and Groom yourself exactly as you want to be perceived: Anyone who tells you that you can't judge a book by its cover is missing the fact that if the cover doesn't look good, no one will open it. As a salesperson, your image creates an impression that influences all aspects of your customer interaction. If you want to sound smarter, seem more trustworthy, be perceived more credibly, then let your dress and grooming represent those things.

OPPORTUNITY

Talent is a myth, effort is what makes salespeople successful:

In business, sports, life, and the profession of selling, talent matters much less than effort applied to the mastery of the skills that lead to success. Those who succeed outwork those who don't every time. Because effort is a choice, we all can be successful in sales.

Call to Action: Opportunity

Today:

Take the next ten minutes and identify the one sales fundamental you feel needs the most improvement. Study it and implement what you learn into today's sales calls. Remember weaknesses can become strengths. If you do this activity you will increase your sales.

NETWORKING

**This One Principle
Can Help You
Lift The Lid On Your Success**

According to John Maxwell, leadership ability is the lid that determines a person's level of success. The lower an individual's ability to lead, the lower the lid on their potential. The higher the individual's ability to lead, the higher the lid on their potential. To give you an example, if your leadership

NETWORKING

rates an 8, then your effectiveness can never be greater than a 7. If your leadership is only a 4, then your effectiveness will be no higher than a 3. Your leadership ability—for better or for worse—always determines your effectiveness and the potential impact on your organization.

In 1937, t wo young brothers named Dick and Maurice opened a small drive-in restaurant in Pasadena, California, located just east of Glendale, and it was a great success. In 1940, they decided to move the operation to San Bernardino, a working-class boomtown fifty miles east of Los Angeles. Their business exploded. Annual sales reached $200,000.

In 1948, their intuition told them that times were changing, and they made modifications to their restaurant business. They streamlined everything. They reduced their menu and focused on selling hamburgers. They created what they called the Speedy Service System making their kitchen into an assembly line with each employee focused on service with speed. The brothers' goal was to fill

NETWORKING

each customer's order in thirty seconds or less. And they succeeded. By the mid-1950s, annual revenue hit $350,000, and by then, Dick and Maurice split net profits of about $100,000 each year.

Who were these brothers? Dick and Maurice McDonald. They hit the great American jackpot, but they never went any further because their weak leadership put a lid on their ability to succeed.

The McDonald brothers' genius was in customer service and kitchen organization. That talent led to the creation of a new system of food and beverage service. But in 1952, when they tried marketing the McDonald's concept, their effort was a dismal failure. The reason was simple. They lacked the leadership necessary to make a larger enterprise effective. Dick and Maurice were good single-restaurant owners. They understood how to run a business, make their systems efficient, cut costs, and increase profits. They were efficient managers. But they were not leaders. Their thinking patterns clamped a lid down on what they could do and become. At the height of their success, Dick and Maurice found themselves smack-dab against the Law of the Lid.

In 1954, the brothers teamed up with a man named Ray Kroc. As soon as he visited the store, he had a vision for its potential. In his mind he could see the restaurant going nationwide in hundreds of markets. He soon struck a deal with Dick and Maurice, and in 1955, he formed McDonald's Systems, Inc. (later called the McDonald's Corporation).

The leadership lid in Ray Kroc's life was sky high. Between 1955 and 1959, Kroc succeeded in opening a hundred restaurants. Four years after that, there were five hundred McDonald's. In 1961, for the sum of $2.7 million, Kroc bought the exclusive rights to McDonald's from the brothers, and he proceeded to turn it into an American institution and global entity.

I believe that success is within the reach of just about everyone, but I also believe that personal success without leadership ability brings only limited effectiveness. Without leadership ability, a person's impact is only a fraction of what it could

NETWORKING

be with good leadership. Whatever you will accomplish is restricted by your ability to lead others.

Call to Action: Networking

Today:

Take the next fifteen minutes and call someone in your network that you feel is a good leader. Ask them how they have developed their leadership skills. Ask them what books they have read, the seminars they have attended, or the strategist they have hired. They will be honored that you think of them as a leader. If you will do this activity you will not only build a deeper relationship with the person you call, you will also learn how to be a more effective leader which will raise the lid of your success.

ENTREPRENEURSHIP

Are You Alice In Wonderland Or Are You Wile E. Coyote?

When Alice was lost in Wonderland, she met the Cheshire Cat and exchanged this dialogue with him:
"Would you tell me, please, which way I ought to go from here?' 'That depends a good deal on where you want to get to,' said the Cat.
'I don't much care where' said Alice. 'Then it doesn't matter which way you go,' said the Cat."

ENTREPRENEURSHIP

As entrepreneurs, if we are not focused on our objective, we don't know where we are going. We become a "yes" man or woman to everyone we meet. We have no true purpose to our actions or direction. Do you know where you are going? Sometimes we don't, and that is okay, but there are other times we don't know because we don't plan. The old adage, "If you fail to plan you plan to fail" is still true today.

Contrast Alice with Wile E. Coyote. Every day the Coyote knew exactly what he wanted. It was the

ENTREPRENEURSHIP

Roadrunner. Each day he had a new plan. If one plan failed, it didn't stop him, he was prepared to start something new. Which one would you rather be? Alice—lost in the woods—or Coyote, in a constant pursuit of your passion?

Call to Action: Entrepreneurship

Today:

Take the next fifteen minutes and create your "Coyote" plan for today. Explore new ideas. Try a different angle on an old problem. Change the direction of your chase. Remember the definition of insanity is doing the same thing over and over again expecting different results. If you will do this activity you are guaranteed to get new results.

---- YOU ----

Your Past Does Not Represent Your Future If You Will Do This One Thing

David Neeleman knows the challenges of overcoming failure. He dropped out of college to pursue his discount travel company. Within a year, he filed bankruptcy and was out of business. He then went to work at a travel agency to find out what he had done wrong and how to better operate his next venture. The next ten years involved a lot of ups

---| YOU |---

and downs. Neeleman started a small discount airline in Salt Lake City, Utah. Within a couple of years, Southwest Airlines bought out his company, and he was a multi-millionaire. Southwest hired him back but then fired him within five months.

Neeleman was not deterred. In due time, he started another airline named Jet Blue. For most airline companies, now is not the time to expand or to start new operations. Jet Blue is not like most companies. Since its inception, Jet Blue has grown rapidly. It offers discount travel on a fleet of new planes. In 2005, it was ranked first in the annual Airline Quality Ranking. Not bad for a failure and dropout.

Whether you have been fired, dropped out of school, or have had financial setbacks, no one owns your future but you. If your life has been affected by the economy, and you feel like you will never be able to turn it around, consider the following people who declared bankruptcy. This did not stop them from recovering and contributing back to society.

YOU

- Samuel L. Clemens (Mark Twain)
- Walt Disney
- Francis Ford Coppola
- William Fox, co-founder of 20th Century Fox Corp
- Ulysses S. Grant
- Larry King
- Gary Kurtz, Producer of Star Wars and American Graffiti
- Donald Trump
- P.T. Barnum
- Henry John Heinz
- Henry Ford
- Rembrandt
- Mozart
- L. Frank Baum, Author of Wizard of Oz
- Milton Hershey
- Charles Goodyear
- Thomas Jefferson

Your past does not represent your future if you create a clear plan. This one simple technique will

YOU

undo years of mistakes. Do not back down from a challenge. You have untapped internal strength. You are the only one who can write the next chapter of your life. Have courage and be faithful. Our greatest tragedies can turn into our greatest triumphs.

Call to Action: You

Today:

Take the next fifteen minutes and write your own future. Be detailed: describe your family, the types of cars you will drive, the home you will live in, the philanthropy you will do, and the business you will have. Remember your past does not predict your future. If you do this activity you will have the ability to create the future you desire.

www.ingramcontent.com/pod-product-compliance
Lightning Source LLC
Chambersburg PA
CBHW021133300426
44113CB00006B/415